ROBERT MANGOLD

COLUMN STRUCTURE PAINTINGS

FEBRUARY 9–MARCH 10, 2007

PACEWILDENSTEIN

545 WEST 22ND STREET NEW YORK NY 10011

CURVES EVOLVE

Richard Shiff

Idea/image

> If painting deteriorates into the making of beautiful things, clever things, shocking things, funny things, lecturing things and its cousin preaching things, at the expense of deep-felt experience and concentrated seeing, then looking at gallery shows will be no more involving than using a remote control on [multichannel] cable TV.
> —Robert Mangold, 1994[1]

> I think the idea of trying to find wholeness is no longer relevant....I think incompleteness is what we are.
> —Robert Mangold, 2006[2]

Robert Mangold sets his art to its own channel. Not much else resembles his work; and he rarely, if ever, alludes to an idea or an image as prerequisite to grasping the essence of his practice, whether the object in question is a single painting or the entirety of one of his series. Facing his work, you are already seeing and thinking; you have the idea and the image. Your reservoir of ordinary experience provides any supplemental information you may need: what a wall is, what a column is, the connotations of horizontality and verticality, the gravitational sense of up and down. You lack only the certainties no painting and not even life can offer. This is the "incompleteness" factor to which Mangold alludes; he acknowledges that no work of art can make a person whole, satisfying every psychic, emotional, and aesthetic need. But a work can point to its missing parts, indicating directions available for experience to take.

"Beautiful things, clever things, shocking things…": in Mangold's estimation, these varieties of contemporary art lose their experiential value. Each has its special way of convincing a viewer of its accomplished finality, as if it were presenting its information or its effect with nothing missing. Attributes of this sort, even including "beautiful," do not suit Mangold's art.[3] Take the example of *Column Structure IX*, 2006 (p. 37). It conjoins an internal orthogonal grid with arabesques of linear figures and a lopsided external shape, all developing from the painter's involvement with the perception of verticality. This quasi-architectural painting is too strange, but also too bold and direct, to seem "beautiful." Yet its form is neither aggressive nor transgressive enough to "shock," and rationality lies behind its look. As the most expansive example of the Column Structure series to

fig. 1
Barnett Newman
Ulysses, 1952
oil and Magna on canvas, 11' 1/2" x 4' 2 1/8"
The Menil Collection, Houston
© 2007 Barnett Newman Foundation/Artist Rights Society (ARS), New York

date, this one, Mangold decided, should be colored a light yellow to avoid an impression of massiveness.[4] The external shape of *Column Structure IV*, 2006 (p. 27) is comparably odd but gives an impression of relative slenderness; Mangold chose to color it a warm, rather heavy yellow. One yellow is bright, brittle, acidic, perhaps airy; the other (at least by contrast) is dense, sweet, mineral-like, even earthy. Just as "beauty" misses the mark of these works, it would be wrong to call them "clever" as an acknowledgment of their sophisticated coordination of color and shape. This would imply that Mangold was performing visual trickery, perhaps capitalizing slyly on some established theory of form and color. Where is the trick? What theory? You tell me, the artist might reply. He would insist that intuition is his source and guide. *Column Structure IX* and *Column Structure IV* merely do what they do. Whatever questions these works answer will not be found on the cable channel of some artist, critic, or theorist. The "meaning" of this art is an unknown that Mangold's activity continues to bring forth through additional variations on the type—his type.

"I think that paintings are answers," Mangold once said, "answers for which no question has been asked."[5] The statement may be "clever" in a colloquial sense, but the works to which it refers are far more than clever. I think of paintings such as *Column Structure VII*, 2006 (p. 33): its shape flares outward at the top, but also, in a less pronounced way, at the bottom. Mangold intended his Column Structure series, as well as the Column Painting series that preceded it, to test the possibilities of a vertical format at large scale. The idea came to him from an image—Barnett Newman's *Ulysses* (fig. 1)—reproduced on the invitation to an exhibition.[6] Newman's painting caused Mangold to reflect on the prevalence of horizontal formats in his own previous work, and how a pronounced, even exaggerated, vertical could introduce a new and challenging dimension. Most of the full-size Column Structures reach a height of ten feet, as do the Column Paintings. (*Column Structure I*, 2005 [p. 19] is somewhat taller, and some of the Column Paintings reach twelve feet.) Perhaps while working at his sketchpad, Mangold intuited that a Column Structure could be extended and expanded at its base as well as at its top. With its image, *Column Structure VII* probes this variation on the fundamental idea; *Column Structure XII*, 2006 (p. 43) does the same thing more expressly.[7] The degree to which an image conforms to an idea (or an idea to an image) is indeterminate: a theoretical crux that Mangold's process of art, both the thinking and the making, renders experiential and concrete. Still, his works answer no questions. More likely, they create questions that call for more response than their example ever provides. Continuity of work is the only reasonable answer. Keep on thinking and looking.

fig. 2
Agnes Martin
Little Children Playing with Love, 2001
acrylic and graphite on canvas, 60 x 60"
Private collection
© 2007 Agnes Martin / Artist Rights Society (ARS), New York

Mangold's paintings are stealth art. Physically distinct, yet without obvious semiotic connections, they get noticed but never cry out for attention. They neither joke around nor articulate theoretical claims. Their forms are radical but stage no programmatic cultural intervention. This art cannot be read like a lecture for the information it may convey, a politics it may promote, or a moral truth it may instill. It does not reduce to humor, irony, advocacy, or provocation. Despite all these exclusions—the exclusion of artistic pretentiousness in its multiple guises—the purpose of art, the nature of its social and cultural engagement, concerns Mangold, who writes on this issue compellingly, occasionally bringing his succinctly formulated thoughts before a public audience. His statement of 1994 ("If painting deteriorates…") was an instance of thinking by writing. Probably not intended for any reader but himself, it remained unpublished until 2000. There, Mangold warns of the leftover strategies of modernism and postmodernism being swept away in a tide of cultural and commercial philistinism.

Consistent with his rejection of the attribute "beauty," Mangold has little interest in spontaneity or technical panache. He covers his large canvases rapidly, but not because he engages them while in a creative fury or flurry. One rational aim is to spread a full coat of acrylic color before it dries, to avoid leaving visible overlaps of the roller. The use of a roller itself facilitates speed and inhibits development of the type of personalized touch that Mangold would regard as an irrelevant distraction. Speed also leads to a desired degree of uniformity; but this is hardly an absolute, for Mangold's technique tolerates significant variation in the density of the surface color. He also works quickly to avoid lingering over details: "I want to approach the final painting with a clear idea of what must happen....In a sense I become the painting assistant when I'm painting. I'm not really making aesthetic decisions....I'm just absorbed in the most technical of things and then [only later] I sit back and think about the work, look at it."[8] Agnes Martin represents a parallel case. Mangold's technique is the more complicated, but it recalls hers because of the use of black pencil coupled with thin acrylic washes of luminous color, a most basic combination of materials (see Martin, *Little Children Playing with Love*, 2001 [fig. 2]). Both artists apply paint as if the main thing were just to get the job done: no fuss.[9] They take "painting"—a show of rarefied professionalism—out of the practice of painting. Mangold intends "to paint the surface [as if] painting a real wall in a loft or apartment, no more or less artful than this."[10]

So Mangold's painting keeps "painting" to a minimum. But he thinks a lot. He prepares. He thinks *through* the preparation for each work. This holds true in a double sense: on the one hand, thinking things out in advance; on the other hand, allowing the process of making to supply additional ideas. Mangold is able to verbalize much of this thinking—in fact, he is adept at it—but his judgments are intuitive and often without analytical backup.[11] Each painting articulates the artist's thought yet is materially specific and apart from whatever words and sketchpad configurations may have preceded it. In the Column Structure series, between a study at two-thirds scale and a final version, intuition may have intervened so that the color differs. When Mangold has completed a full-scale painting, it is as if the same thinking that not only led to it but also guided it along its course now must catch up with it. Between the idea and the image, the link between thinking and making, making and thinking, is a feeling of *need*. It drives both impulses (thinking and making). This need is an emotional condition that remains a living constant: "I create and shape my work to satisfy my needs," Mangold wrote in 1993. "This does not mean that I am two people, one who needs and one who makes; there is only one person. [It is] a whole process, this needing and making."[12]

Each of us is one, but each is also two: one who feels a need, and one who responds to it. We have a feeling: perhaps sensory, perhaps emotional. At its core the distinction remains uncertain, as in the case of thinking and seeing. Mangold's attitude toward his art—evident to him whenever he steps back to reflect on his thoughts and feelings—raises classical philosophical problems concerning communicative expression in one medium (verbalization) as opposed to expression in another medium (visualization). Images compete with words for our limited attention. Mangold probes the relation between verbal thinking and actions guided by the eye. Perhaps for him, this very endeavor represents the emotional need that haunts his being, a need to escape stereotype and all definitive categorization, to strive toward intellectual, perceptual, and sensory wholeness in a culture that has forsaken the aim: "I think the potential crisis is in the loss of belief in Art…[the abandonment of] painting as a meaningful instrument of self-awareness and discovery, of invention and revelation. It is a loss of faith in painting's ability to speak and the viewer's ability to see."[13]

"To speak…to see": significantly, Mangold's formulation alludes to verbalization as well as visualization, and each expressive mode becomes a metaphor for the other. As evidence of success in seeing, we accept a convincing verbal account of what has been seen, as if a verbal formulation were needed to complete the act of vision. (This is not a question of community. If you have no second party with whom to test a judgment, you will conduct a dialogue with yourself regarding what you've seen.) In Mangold's case, the visual brings its own satisfactions, even if these successes never eliminate the need to move on, which is often expressed in verbal language. His philosophical stakes resemble those of Henri Bergson: "Numerous systems of disjoining, of fragmenting [experience] are possible; but no system corresponds to the clear linkages, the utter connect-edness of reality."[14] No system—visual, verbal, whatever—organizes all of reality, gets everything in a proper, satisfying order. As we continue to live, bumps in our experience are the proof of this.

Mangold has faith in the fullness and connectedness of Bergson's "reality"; pragmatically, however, he acknowledges that he lives in a disjointed world of psychic fragmentation. Every action is only a part of the action that could have been, the event that might have occurred. His paintings are impulsive responses to the felt demands of the moment. Even exceptional artists rise only so far above this human condition. Mangold's need is to create an art that captures the sense of experiential wholeness, even as he acknowl-edges (especially in written reflections) that his inventive creations are but imperfect parts of the wholeness he still fails to understand. If he were to let his painting "lecture" or "preach," he would be solving—no, pretending to solve—the problem of part and whole, separation and connection. He would be allowing one mode (the verbal) to dominate all others, reaching its formulaic conclusions. Left behind, the visual image would have no reciprocal effect on the triumphant verbal idea. This is the deceptive "wholeness" that Mangold rejects, the theoretical antithesis of the "incompleteness" he endures.

Not long ago, in September 2004, Mangold spoke at the Modern Art Museum of Fort Worth. His topic, as he referred to it, was "this whole mysterious process."[15] He knows that, despite its transparency, its openness, his painting is as much a mystery to him as it is to anyone else. Not only does a completed work introduce effects unforeseen in the planning, the very words used to formulate the situation introduce additional problems that cannot be ignored. This holds for the most essential terms, an indication of the philosophical depth of the painter's dilemma, the "mystery." Like many words, *painting* is a verb that signifies a process as well as a noun that signifies its product. Just as those who create writings are writers, Mangold must be a "painter," if only because his process creates paintings: "When I meet someone who asks what I do, I say, 'I'm a painter.'"[16] He cannot say simply "I'm an artist," for this would provoke a follow-up—What kind?—and he would be back in the same corner, identifying himself with the medium of painting. He resists the simplicity of this association because any particular painting is only a part of the whole known by the same inadequate name. It is the effect without all the additional factors that constitute its cause: elements of the artist's life. To identify art solely with its medium amounts to an unacceptable shortcut (like pursuing paths of "beauty," "shock," and so on), a circumvention of the mystery.

I might argue that painting (or any mode of art) never fully satisfies an emotional need because the need encapsulates it; painting itself is the painter's emotional condition. A painter cannot get outside of painting. The process that Mangold understands as his kind of painting includes thinking, sketching, and testing. The thoughts he composed for his Fort Worth lecture—these too were elements of his painting, "this whole mysterious process." An individual painting, like a day's planning or even a day's lecturing, does no more than provide temporary emotional relief, a relaxation of the artist's creative tension. This is mere speculation on my part. But the line of thinking gains credence from the fact that Mangold works in series and is uncomfortable—creatively dislocated—during the periods between the completion of one series and his settling into, committing himself to, the next: "These transitions are always a time of insecurity and turmoil."[17]

Writers can think coherently with the very words, the same syntax, the same structures that form their writing. But can painters think with lines, shapes, and colors? They draw lines, build shapes, lay down colors. Is this thinking? Or is it an action that occurs between the thoughts that set it in motion and those that sustain it? Mangold's contemporary Richard Serra, also committed to abstract art, has argued that a sketchpad is conceivably a corpus of thoughts: "To draw a line is to have an idea."[18] His syntax implies that the act of drawing precedes formulation of the idea.

For Mangold, thought is preparatory, but it also comes after the fact. "I spend time," he told his Fort Worth audience, "probably more time than I should, trying to understand this activity I'm involved in, how my work happens." His attempt to understand is verbal but has its grounding in a viewing process: "I often sit for hours looking at paintings I have done, or am doing, day after day. What am I looking at?"[19]

It would be a shame if such questioning of inventive images were followed with verbal clichés, and inadequate, stale ideas. How does thinking move beyond its *ideés reçues*? How does it take a form other than the ones already imprinted? Long ago, the dramatist Heinrich von Kleist ventured an answer: "The idea comes in speaking… [The medium of expression] is not…a drag chain on the mind, but a second wheel running parallel to it on the same axle."[20] If two wheels move on the same axle, then both determine the direction of motion. So it may be that thinking and looking occur simultaneously. At any given moment, however, consciousness attends only to one of them. This would explain a certain confusion or indeterminateness that Mangold sometimes expresses, for want of a better solution, by the compound term *idea/image*: "I work in groups of work that

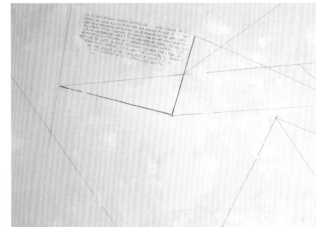

explore an idea/image…[It] seems to come not from the outside world but from some interior world, as there are certain formal and visual needs that must be personal and are not explainable in any way….They are like an itch that must be scratched."[21] Wisely, Mangold realizes that he cannot—no, he *can* (we all do), but he knows that he *ought* not—separate the idea from the image, the thought from its associated expression. Every work is not only a scratch, but also an itch, and for an artist, itching (thinking) and scratching (making) are both self-stimulating: "In my work the idea is more image-generated than the image is idea-generated. The work satisfies a need, the way scratching satisfies an itch. And in the same way that scratching often does not completely satisfy the itch, the work does not completely satisfy the need. But it propels you along."[22] This is an instance of connectedness, whether in life or in art. Mangold's statement evokes a continuity of the working process, with no completion. It also suggests a continuity of creative tension, which will find no lasting emotional release.

As Mangold often states, his "paintings build from each other," and "the work generates more work."[23] This may be true of all inventive artists. With Mangold, however, it becomes all the more true as he shifts between idea and image, attending to these realms of experience and expression as equals—separate, indeterminately related, but equal in significance. He tends to focus on how inseparable these very separate parts of the "whole mysterious process" are at any given moment: "From my experience, I cannot be the maker and the viewer at the same time. When I am working I am watching the working, but I am not a viewer or reader of what I have done until I stop, back up, change roles and become the viewer/reader."[24] The viewer/reader is the person with ideas; the maker is the person with images. Two in one, one in two.

In 1975 Mangold and his wife, painter Sylvia Plimack Mangold, moved to a farm in Washingtonville, New York, where they continue to live and have their studios. Sol LeWitt, their friend of many years, constructed a drawing in the new home, keying its primary elements, a right angle and an arc, to two existing nail holes in the plastered wall that would bear it [fig. 3]. On the wall itself, LeWitt inscribed verbal instructions for locating and composing the two linear elements. To read these texts—clear, precise, yet utterly confusing to eye and mind—is to realize that verbalization remains disjoined from the visualization to which it corresponds. LeWitt has stated his concern to "redirect the emphasis to idea rather than [material] effect."[25] With his wall drawing for the Mangold family, he demonstrated an indirect corollary, something Mangold himself repeatedly learns from his own working experience: visual effects of an inventive sort do not lend themselves to concise description. Coordinate word and image seamlessly and you produce a cliché.

fig. 4
Robert Mangold
Red Section, 1963
oil on fiberboard, 92 5/8 x 48 5/8"
Portland Art Museum, Oregon. Gift of Ed Cauduro

fig. 5
Robert Mangold
Red Wall, 1965
oil on masonite, 96 1/2 x 96 1/2"
Tate. Lent by the American Fund for the Tate Gallery 2006

Imagine that "thinking" can occur in a more primitive form than what we usually experience as either idea or image. To be manifest as more than a vague emotion, more than the need that Mangold suspects must underlie his aesthetic practice, this inchoate mode of thought would have to develop accessibility and articulation. Such conversion of primitive emotional energy might occur in the field of creative fantasy: part poetic verbalization, part artistic visualization. This sense of fantasy, like Mangold's sense of intuition, has pragmatic value. In its role as psychic mediator, fantasy would grant to images and ideas equal emotional and intellectual status. Along with Mangold's thoughts come images of feeling, not as resolutions of his emotional need, but as extensions of the feeling that belongs specifically to the form of his thought, its emotional unfolding, its evolution.[26]

Fragment

> I suddenly got this idea…that the paintings should continue, that the painting should be a fragment, a part of a rhythm, part of a structure that is continuous, that *could* be continuous anyway, where you're seeing enough to know what the structure is.
> —Robert Mangold, 2006[27]

Mangold refers to his Column images as fragments that are apart from, as well as part of, the rest of the visual environment. With the exception of the earliest members of the Column Painting series, each Column Painting and Column Structure appears to begin and end arbitrarily at its outer edges. This effect stems not only from the wave-like repetition of the curving linear elements, but also from the fact that Mangold allows the organizing grids to remain manifest as penciled lines: "The grid allows you to see the regularity [the intervals] of the repeating curve."[28] By their nature, grids extend and expand. Mangold's grids are more than mere guidelines for his drawing linear figures; they become guides for the viewer as well, clues as to how the entire work is structured. Or, more than that, they represent a structure in tension with the figure that depends on this same structural grid, rather like a thyrsus (a vertical rod supporting a spiraling vine). Mangold's grid units could be extended—"*could* be continuous"—but they are not.[29] Just as a grid, theoretically, is limitless, so any material instantiation of a grid has its pragmatic limitations. Here, the image—say, the specific painting *Column Structure XI*, 2006 (p. 41), with its nod to horizontality as it makes its ten-foot ascent—seems to limit

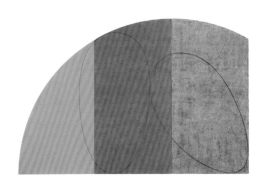

fig. 6
Robert Mangold
1/2 W Series, 1968
acrylic and black pencil on masonite, 48 x 96"
The Museum of Modern Art, New York. Larry Aldrich Foundation

fig. 7
Robert Mangold
Curved Plane/Figure VIII, 1995
acrylic and black pencil on canvas, 8' 2" x 12' 3"
Private collection

the conceptual idea while simultaneously opening this idea to limitless variations, each of them nevertheless confined to a particular configuration.

For whatever reason, Mangold has long been aware of the incompleteness of images: this, despite the fact that it is the very nature of an image to be whole at the moment of its appearance. Experientially, it ought to be whole, for what you see is what you see; there is no more of it. In Mangold's words, "What is there is all there."[30] But once you begin to link images or views with what you already know of the world, they become fragments. Ideas fragment images. Mangold has often associated the fragmentary nature of views with the Lower Manhattan environment that inspired many of his works of the 1960s (he moved there in 1962): "I would see everything in fragments, in sections—the section of a truck, the section of a building. [In New York] you don't see the total, but the fragment becomes its own kind of total."[31] His thinking—the word *fragment* itself—seems to have solidified the nature of his viewing.

Mangold's early abstractions pushed the sense of image-incompleteness to extremes. *Red Section* (1963 [fig. 4]) looks as if it were part of a huge graphic form, like outdoor commercial signage or advertising. It is Pop art without the characteristic literalness, legibility, and wholeness, a connotation of urban commercialism that (perhaps thankfully) provides no actual goods. *Red Wall* (1965 [fig. 5]) is a more radical work, fragmented in a different way by its evocation of walls, window framing, and other familiar architectural elements. It is none of these "real" things, but also not quite wholly itself, because the smaller rectilinear shapes set into (removed from) its two adjoined panels look as if they might be the beginnings of something else. Such multivalent work prepared Mangold to pursue his fragmentation idea with various kinds of images that could claim both completeness and incompleteness. In 1968, he constructed *1/2 W Series* (fig. 6), one of a number of related masonite panels, each with a distinct but ambivalent external shape: "A half-circle is a complete shape despite the implication that it's not a complete shape....This is very much a part of the content of the work...this sense of completeness and incompleteness—or perhaps the impossibility of completeness."[32] During the 1990s, he returned to half circles and other, more eccentric radial fragments, such as *Curved Plane/Figure VIII* (fig. 7), in which a "missing" right-hand segment of the lunette seems both there and not there.

With certain paintings of the late 1980s, such as *Green Tilted Ellipse/Gray Frame* (1989 [fig. 8, p. 14]), Mangold approached fragmentation and incompleteness by juxtaposing two configured elements that were as far

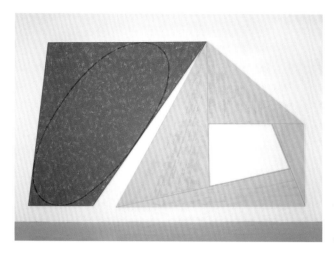

fig. 8
Robert Mangold
Green Tilted Ellipse/Gray Frame, 1989
acrylic and black pencil on canvas, 8' 5" x 13' 11"

14   from resembling one another as proved manageable. He attempted to associate the disparate forms so that they (just barely) complemented each other. This rendered the work whole even as its components remained apart, as disjunctive fragments. The two elements were at once complete (as one) and incomplete (as two). Mangold explained: "I wanted to have these almost opposing structures, joined at one edge or even at only one point, make a single work. It was this struggle between the separation and unity that interested me."[33] He was encouraged in this venture by the example of Picasso's *Demoiselles d'Avignon*, with its disparate styles of representation within a single composition: "It has so many different types of painting going on."[34] He also noted Barnett Newman's ink drawings of the late 1940s.[35] *Untitled (The Break)* (1946 [fig. 9]) is a prime example; every detail of the brushed and taped marking seems just a bit too removed from every other detail. Its central wedge of light can be read as a negative break as much as a positive join and may have inspired the one-point connection that *Green Tilted Ellipse/Gray Frame* dared to make.

However else they may operate, the curving lines of Mangold's Column Paintings play an active game of uniting and disuniting their elements. The grid of *Column Painting 16* (2004 [fig. 10, p. 16]) segments the vertical rectangle into thirds to guide the course of a curve that repeats its wave three times: from the center bottom to the left edge, then back around to the right edge, then to the left edge again, then terminating (or not) back at the center. The grid also marks off halves and quarters to guide the other two wave forms, both of which repeat twice but are otherwise out of phase, as if each were a tide or a moon, one "full" when the other is "new." To see the three curves as a single pattern is a struggle, although at times it may be possible. More likely, the curves will generate a complicated counterpoint to be extended at either end. When the wave-like curves meet at both ends of the "column," as in *Column/Figure 18* (2004 [fig. 11, p. 16]), a single figure more readily emerges from the image drawn in pencil, but it is quite an eccentric one. Following the structural grid, I wonder why a figure formed so simply should look so odd. *Column/Figure 18* consists merely of a wave with four repeats played against a wave with two repeats—intervals of quarters and halves on the grid. It recalls works such as *1/2 W Series (Orange)* and *Curved Plane/Figure VIII*: simple, yet complicated; closed, yet open.

To attribute incompleteness and fragmentation to the external environment (Mangold's sense of Lower Manhattan) or to one's internalized work (from *Red Section* and *Red Wall* to *Column Structure XII*) may represent an unwitting deception, a ruse that distracts from a psychological fact. Mangold's commitment to the idea of the fragment, as well as his persistent image of things as fragmentary, may result (once again)

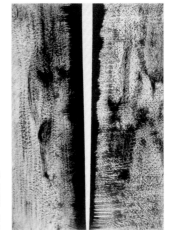

from need. Incompleteness suits this artist's temperament. Although he has the patience to make things whole and is a flawless craftsman, his resistance to closing off possibilities gets the better of any drive toward perfection. All of his questions remain open to ever more answers. He entertains no dogma, has no doxa. Nothing is certain. When Mangold studies his achievements and asks "What am I looking at?" the question is serious.[36] To the extent that his inner emotional need resonates with the emotional valence of others—it does this for me—his work succeeds in addressing its particular moment in history and the social psychology of our time.

Evolution of a curve

Whilst this planet has gone cycling on according to the fixed law of gravity, from so simple a beginning endless forms most beautiful and most wonderful have been, and are being evolved.
—Charles Darwin, 1859 [37]

The evolution [*déroulement*] of psychical life is continuous.
—Henri Bergson, 1908 [38]

"Evolution" in the sense of Bergson's metaphor refers to the unfolding or development of a geometric curve, often implying its straightening or otherwise opening out and extending, revealing itself by undoing itself: literally, "unrolling."[39] As mental and emotional life "unrolls," it neither segments nor fragments; its whole is indivisible. But we reflect on it, analyze it, and, ultimately, understand it in terms of fragmentary visions, memories, and ideas. Darwin's allusion to unrolling (from the concluding sentence of *The Origin of Species*) comes linked to a vision of cycles of planetary motion. It may be that thoughts of Earth's orbit led the scientist to intuit *evolved* as the appropriate final word (its only appearance) in his text. Earth's orbital curve spins out life continuously. And life evolves, unfolds, unrolls.

Immediately before making the Column Paintings and Column Structures, Mangold produced his series of Curled Figures. What curls, uncurls. The tight end of a curl is its involute; the loose (uncurled) end is its evolute. A curling line has a natural limit in that it becomes ever tighter around its center (ever more involved with

fig. 10
Robert Mangold
Column Painting 16, 2004
acrylic and black pencil on canvas
10' 1/4" x 2' 4"
Private collection

fig. 11
Robert Mangold
Column/Figure 18, 2004
acrylic and black pencil on canvas
10' 1/4" x 2'
Private collection

itself, we might say). But an uncurling line becomes looser and more open, without limit (it communicates with the rest of creation). "Evolution" alludes to uncurling. *Curled Figure XXII (Version 2)*, 2002 (fig. 12) has two curls at opposite ends of a single reversing line. Both ends curl counterclockwise but are inverted with respect to one another's positions within a surrounding five-foot square (the painting comprises four square panels, horizontally arrayed). The two end-curls evolve equally, but with another inversion—one evolves to the right, the other evolves to the left. The two evolutions form a single line or figure: two in one, one becoming two. It is a situation of connection/disconnection or whole/fragment of the type that fascinates Mangold. It affirms his inner emotional state. He is at ease with evolute forms, as well as with the more structured involute forms, because he tolerates life's ambiguities and contradictions.

Mangold's curves "evolve" in a number of his Column Structures; like waves, they repeat at intervals, only to turn suddenly away from the columnar core, extending, lengthening into a relatively flattened arc. Such a turn constitutes an evolution. *Column Structure III*, 2006 (p. 25) sets curves of a four-unit interval and a three-unit interval against one another. Each demonstrates its basic wave cycle, or perhaps half a cycle, because neither curve completes itself symmetrically by reversing its left/right orientation within the column. Instead of reversing, each curve unfolds in a horizontal direction. Once this happens, no particular cycle is evident although one may be implied, for Mangold leaves the evolution of each curve inconclusive, as an evolution ought to be. The curves are plainly there, structured by the grid yet without suggesting any easy description. Each is set against the greenish gray "ground" of the column. Here, too, description fails. I hesitate to refer to a pictorial ground in the usual way; Mangold's monochromatic plane lies neither behind the curve-figures illusionistically nor beneath them materially. It is a limbo plane, neither definitively below nor definitively above. The painter's technique thoroughly integrates figure, grid, plane, and surrounding shape. The effect—for him, typical—can be disorienting in its matter-of-fact pictorial neutrality. To achieve it, he first draws his grid and curves in pencil; then he uses a roller to apply a chosen color (with directional traces remaining); then, with the image secure in its place, he reestablishes the curves in heavy Prismacolor pencil; and, finally, he adds a last wash of acrylic to bond line and color together. Both visually and materially, the distinct elements become one painting.

Column Structure IV, 2006 (p. 27) opposes a two-unit curve to a three-unit curve. The former remains within the vertical core of the "column," repeating its cycle. The latter breaks rank and evolves. *Column Structure VI*,

fig. 12
Robert Mangold
Curled Figure XXII (Version 2), 2002
acrylic and black pencil on canvas
5' x 20'

2006 (p. 31) reveals that the repeating interval of a curve can be fractional in relation to the structure provided by the grid. The single-line curve has a two-and-one-half-unit interval; the double-line curve, more complex still, shows no apparent regularity. Both curves evolve, arcing outward at the top of the column. *Column Structure VIII*, 2006 (p. 35) explores further possibilities; its single-line, two-unit curve repeats twice, then angles out at the top in response to the grid that follows the angled external shape. Conceivably, this evolved curve will retain the organizing interval apparent in the straight part of the column. With its single-line figure, *Column Structure X*, 2006 (p. 39) establishes yet another point of difference, a wave of self-restraint. The cycle of this curve forms a convex arc extending to only half the width of its grid unit. But where the same figure approaches the top of the column, it evolves into an expansive, even flamboyant form, while its companion double-line curve remains faithful to an initial two-unit cycle. With so much variation in what is still a modest number of works within the Column Structure series, Mangold's choices must be arbitrary in relation to any general system—this is to say, they must be intuitive.

An evolved curve goes in the direction it "wants" to go, where it "needs" to go. It is a figure for the artist himself: a person constrained by an environment of which he can see and know only part, and therefore all the more at liberty to experiment and test. With no possibility of definitive results, Mangold's art serves his antidogmatic temperament. Recently, he hit on a telling metaphor: "A close analogy [to the nature of my work] would be to a kind of journey where you only choose directions in small segments....A final destination cannot even be imagined."[40]

Imagination (fantasy) conceives the means of exploration and coordinates idea-fragments with image-fragments. It says nothing about ends.

Richard Shiff is Effie Marie Cain Regents Chair in Art and Director of the Center for the Study of Modernism, The University of Texas at Austin.

Notes

1. Mangold, "Studio Notes, 1993–94" (note dated 21 October 1994), in Richard Shiff, Robert Storr, Arthur C. Danto, Nancy Princenthal, and Sylvia Plimack Mangold, *Robert Mangold* (London: Phaidon, 2000), 167. I thank Caitlin Haskell for invaluable aid in research, Douglas Baxter and Jon Mason for supplying images and archival material, and, especially, Robert Mangold for precise answers to every question. Unless otherwise noted, quoted words and factual details derive from my conversations and written exchanges with Mangold during the period November 2006 through January 2007.

2. Mangold, statement in Marla Prather, "Interview with Robert Mangold" (20 February 2006), *Robert Mangold/Paul Gauguin*, exh. cat. (Paris: Argol, 2006), 34.

3. Mangold usually suspects that when his art is called "beautiful," the word is "trivializing," masking the fact that the viewer remains untouched by what the artist has found challenging; see Mangold, "Studio Notes, 1993–94" (note dated 26 March 1994), in Shiff et al., *Robert Mangold*, 166.

4. Here and elsewhere, my color terminology follows Mangold's; "light yellow" is his description.

5. Mangold, letter to David Carrier, 20 September 1994 (courtesy Robert Mangold and David Carrier).

6. See Mangold's statement in Prather, "Interview with Robert Mangold," 40.

7. According to Mangold, "[*Column Structure XII*] reinforces the idea that the structure can occur at the base of the column as well as the upper sections of the grid."

8. Mangold, statement (October 1988) in *Robert Mangold: Works on Paper*, exh. cat. (Zurich: Annemarie Verna Gallery, 1988), 8; statement in Shirley Kaneda, "Robert Mangold," *Bomb* 76 (Summer 2001): 29.

9. During the early 1960s, Mangold was especially impressed by this quality in the work of Frank Stella.

10. Mangold, statement to the author, 29 August 1998. See also Prather, "Interview with Robert Mangold," 37.

11. An early statement is typical: "I have followed intuitive feelings or hunches. And, in some cases, I do not have a clearly rational justification for the decisions I've made." Mangold, in Rosalind Krauss, "Robert Mangold: An Interview," *Artforum* 12 (March 1974): 36. Intuition may be a fast form of analysis (fast like a scan), so accelerated that the ordinary mode of verbalization (slow like narration) never comprehends it; see Richard Shiff, "Donald Judd: Fast Thinking," *Donald Judd: Late Work*, exh. cat. (New York: PaceWildenstein, 2000), 4–23.

12. Mangold, "Studio Notes, 1993–94" (note dated 26 February 1993), in Shiff et al., *Robert Mangold*, 164.

13. Mangold, "Studio Notes, 1993–94" (note dated 21 October 1994), in Shiff et al., *Robert Mangold*, 167.

14. Henri Bergson, "Le souvenir du présent et la fausse reconnaissance" (1908), *Oeuvres*, ed. André Robinet (Paris: Presses universitaires de France, 1959), 913 (my translation).

15. Mangold, typescript of unpublished lecture (Modern Art Museum of Fort Worth, Texas), 14 September 2004 (courtesy Robert Mangold).

16. Mangold, statement in Kaneda, "Robert Mangold," 31.

17. Mangold, statement in Kaneda, "Robert Mangold," 29.

18. Richard Serra, "About Drawing: An Interview" (interview by Lizzie Borden, 1977), *Richard Serra: Writings, Interviews* (Chicago: University of Chicago Press, 1994), 52.

19. Mangold, "Studio Notes" (note dated July 1992), in Christel Sauer and Urs Raussmüller, *Robert Mangold: Painting as Wall, Werke von 1964 bis 1993*, exh. cat. (Schaffhausen: Hallen für neue Kunst, 1993), 83.

20. Heinrich von Kleist, "On the Gradual Fabrication of Thoughts While Speaking" (1805–6), *An Abyss Deep Enough: Letters of Heinrich von Kleist with a Selection of Essays and Anecdotes*, ed. and trans. Philip B. Miller (New York: Dutton, 1982), 218, 221.

21. Mangold, unpublished lecture, Modern Art Museum of Fort Worth.

22. Mangold, "Notes on Curled Figure" (note dated 2 February 2000), *Robert Mangold: Curled Figure Paintings*, exh. cat. (New York: PaceWildenstein, 2001), 4.

23. Mangold, "Studio Notes" (note dated 10 February 1992), in Sauer and Raussmüller, *Robert Mangold*, 75; Mangold, "Interview with Sylvia Plimack Mangold," in Shiff et al., *Robert Mangold*, 65.

24. Mangold, "Notes on Curled Figure" (undated note), 6.

25. Sol LeWitt, statement to Andrea Miller-Keller, in "Excerpts from a Correspondence, 1981-1983," *Sol LeWitt Wall Drawings 1968-1984*, exh. cat. (Amsterdam: Stedelijk Museum, 1984), 21.

26. As articulated by philosopher Charles Sanders Peirce, "Every operation of the mind, however complex, has its absolutely simple feeling, the emotion of the *tout ensemble.*" Peirce, "A Definition of Feeling" (c. 1906), *Collected Papers*, ed. Charles Hartshorne, Paul Weiss, and Arthur W. Burks, 8 vols. (Cambridge, Mass.: Harvard University Press, 1958–60), 1: 155.

27. Prather, "Interview with Robert Mangold," 41 (original emphasis).

28. Mangold, unpublished lecture, Modern Art Museum of Fort Worth.

29. In this regard, Mangold sometimes refers to Brancusi's *Endless Column*, an idea for a materialized image of indeterminate extent.

30. Mangold, statement (1987), in Shiff et al., *Robert Mangold*, 11.

31. Mangold, statement in David Carrier, "Robert Mangold's 'Gray Window Wall,'" *Burlington Magazine* 138 (December 1996): 826–27. See also Prather, "Interview with Robert Mangold," 35–36.

32. Mangold, in Kaneda, "Robert Mangold," 29.

33. Mangold, in Kaneda, "Robert Mangold," 30.

34. See Nancy Princenthal, "A Survey of the Paintings," in Shiff et al., *Robert Mangold*, 246.

35. Mangold, statement to the author, 26 July 1998.

36. See note 19.

37. Charles Darwin, *The Origin of Species by Means of Natural Selection*, 2 vols. (New York: A. L. Fowle, 1872 [1859]), 2: 306.

38. Henri Bergson, "Le souvenir du présent et la fausse reconnaissance," *Oeuvres*, 913 (my translation).

39. The mathematical operation of evolution is often applied now to computer imaging; an amorphous contour "evolves" into a recognizable, meaningful shape, as if to curve out of one form and into another.

40. Mangold, unpublished lecture, Modern Art Museum of Fort Worth.

COLUMN STRUCTURE I 2005
acrylic and black pencil on canvas, 11' 1" x 6' 6"

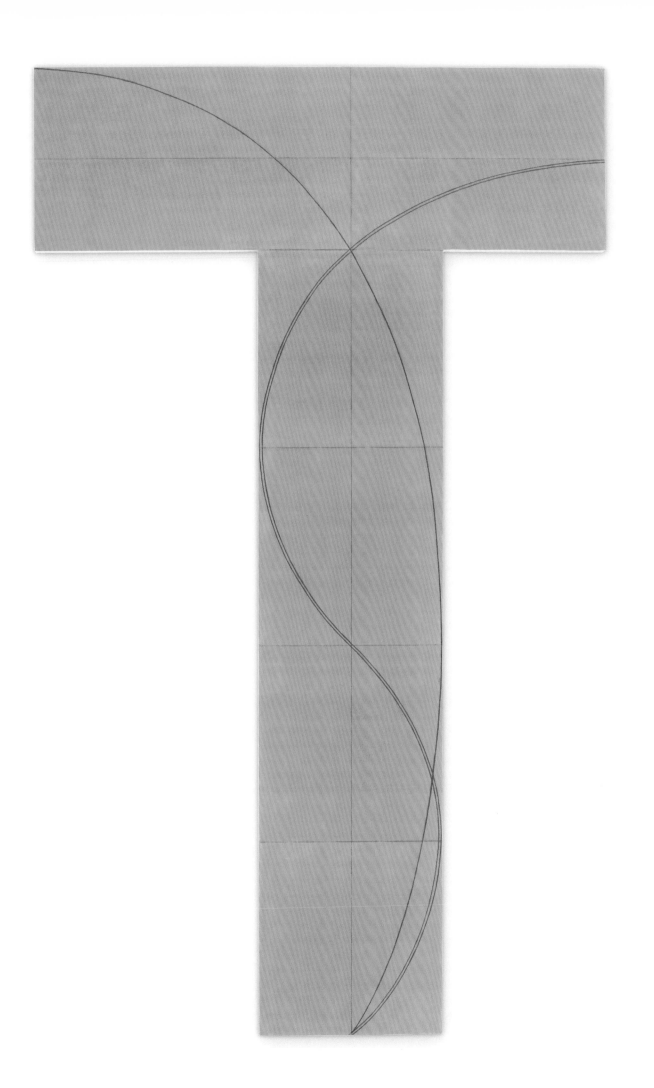

COLUMN STRUCTURE II 2006
acrylic and black pencil on canvas, 10 x 4'

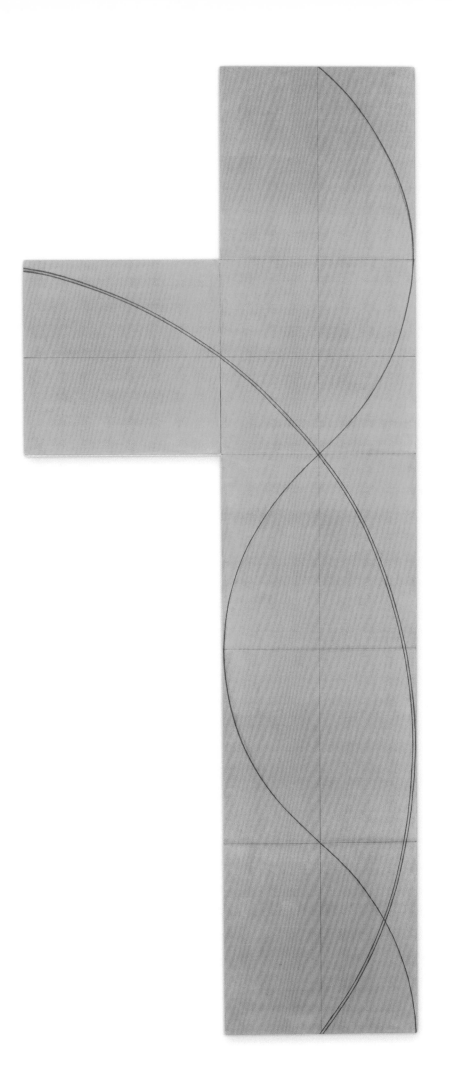

COLUMN STRUCTURE III 2006
acrylic and black pencil on canvas, 10 x 6'

COLUMN STRUCTURE IV 2006
acrylic and black pencil on canvas, 10 x 6'

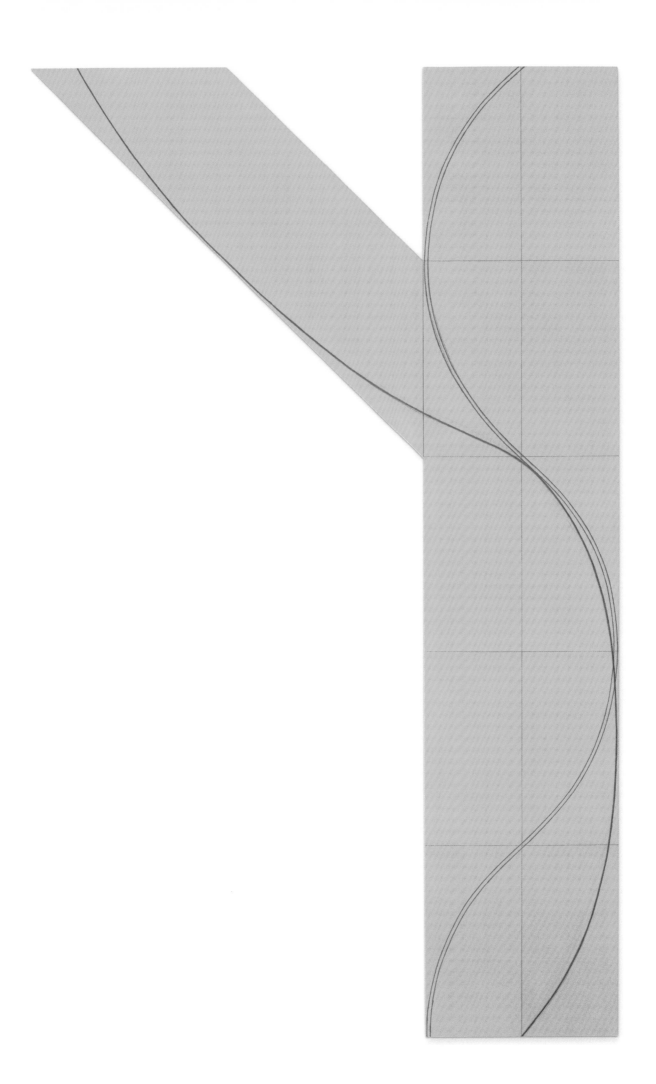

COLUMN STRUCTURE V 2006
acrylic and black pencil on canvas, 10 x 5'

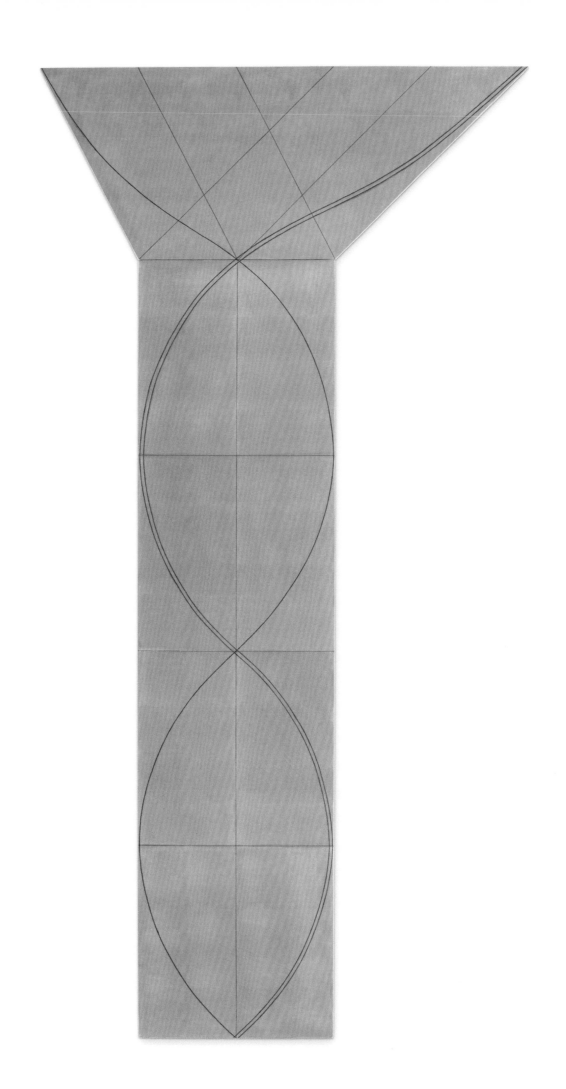

COLUMN STRUCTURE VI 2006
acrylic and black pencil on canvas, 10 x 6'

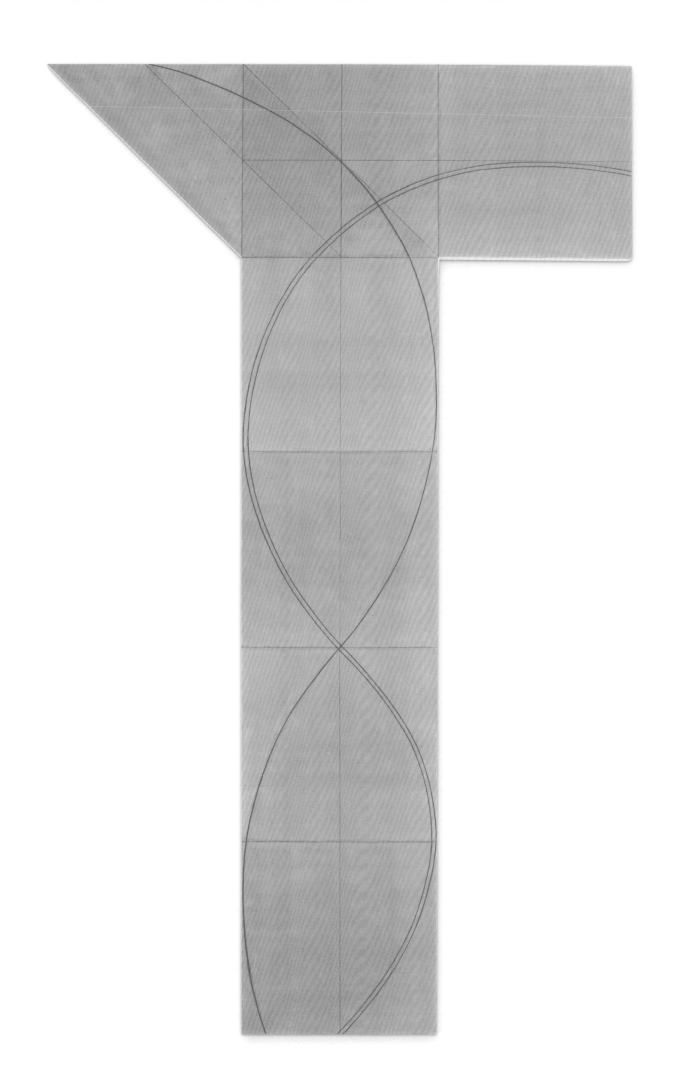

COLUMN STRUCTURE VII 2006
acrylic and black pencil on canvas, 10 x 5'

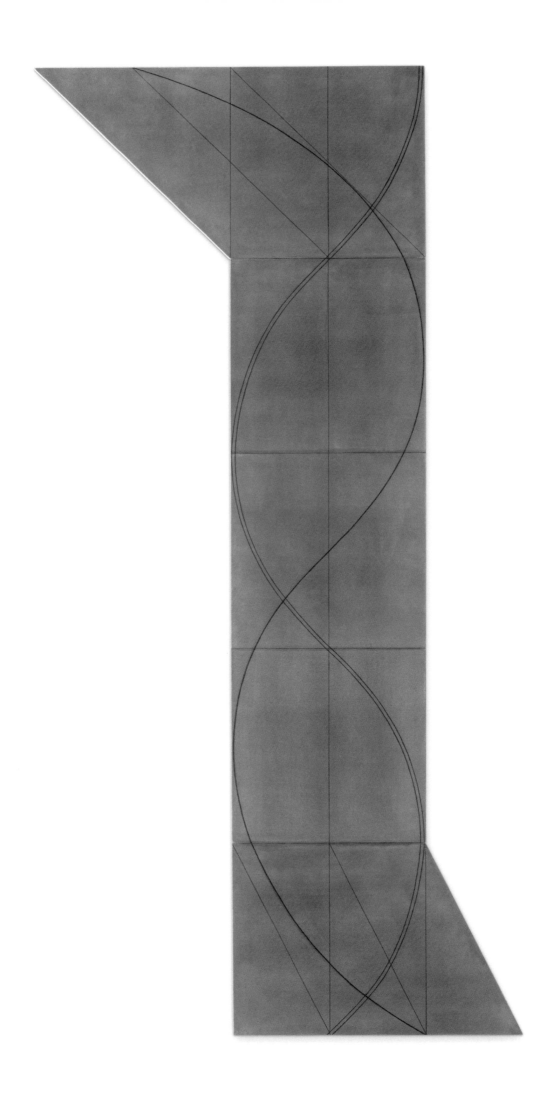

COLUMN STRUCTURE VIII 2006
acrylic and black pencil on canvas, 10 x 5'

COLUMN STRUCTURE IX 2006
acrylic and black pencil on canvas, 10 x 8'

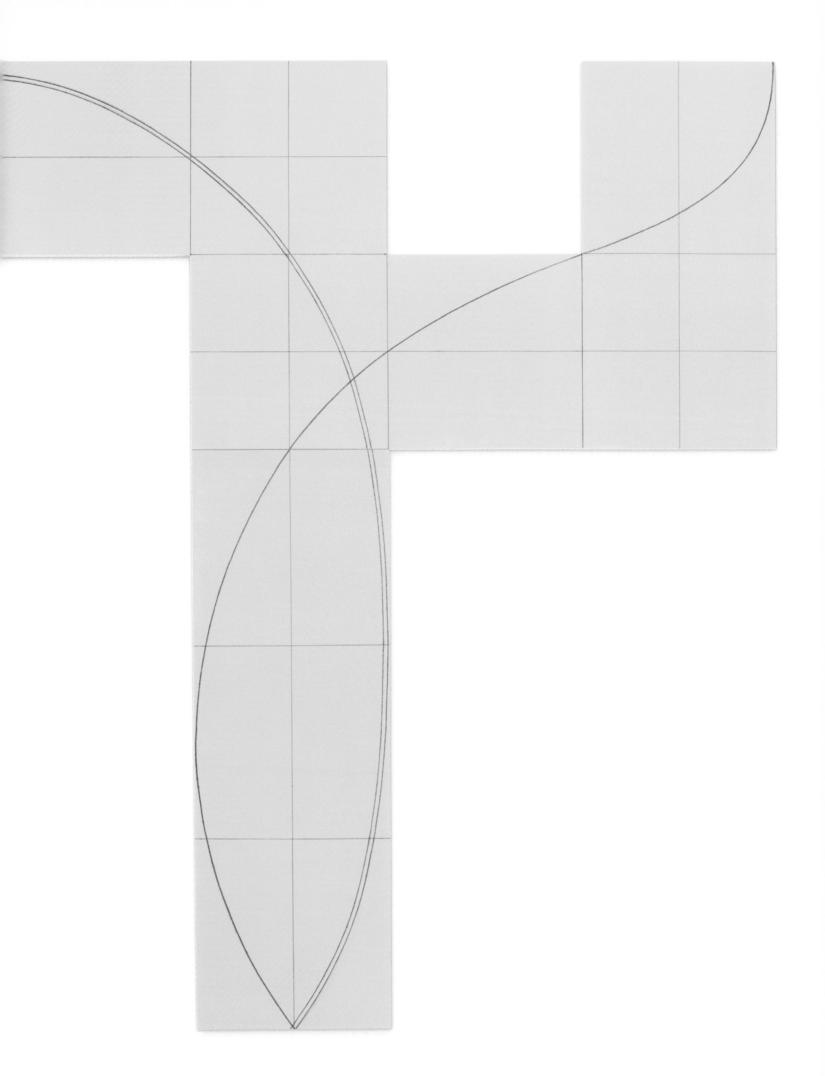

COLUMN STRUCTURE X 2006
acrylic and black pencil on canvas, 10 x 6'

COLUMN STRUCTURE XI 2006
acrylic and black pencil on canvas, 10 x 4'

COLUMN STRUCTURE XII 2006
acrylic and black pencil on canvas, 10 x 6'

CHECKLIST

21   **COLUMN STRUCTURE I** 2005
acrylic and black pencil on canvas, 11' 1" x 6' 6"

23   **COLUMN STRUCTURE II** 2006
acrylic and black pencil on canvas, 10 x 4'
Tate. Presented by the artist 2006

25   **COLUMN STRUCTURE III** 2006
acrylic and black pencil on canvas, 10 x 6'

27   **COLUMN STRUCTURE IV** 2006
acrylic and black pencil on canvas, 10 x 6'

29   **COLUMN STRUCTURE V** 2006
acrylic and black pencil on canvas, 10 x 5'

31   **COLUMN STRUCTURE VI** 2006
acrylic and black pencil on canvas, 10 x 6'

33   **COLUMN STRUCTURE VII** 2006
acrylic and black pencil on canvas, 10 x 5'

35   **COLUMN STRUCTURE VIII** 2006
acrylic and black pencil on canvas, 10 x 5'

37   **COLUMN STRUCTURE IX** 2006
acrylic and black pencil on canvas, 10 x 8'

39   **COLUMN STRUCTURE X** 2006
acrylic and black pencil on canvas, 10 x 6'

41   **COLUMN STRUCTURE XI** 2006
acrylic and black pencil on canvas, 10 x 4'

43   **COLUMN STRUCTURE XII** 2006
acrylic and black pencil on canvas, 10 x 6'

Cover:
Column Structure V, 2006 (detail)

Photography:
Digital Image © The Museum of Modern Art/Licensed by SCALA/Art Resource, New York; p. 13 (fig. 6)
Jacques Faujour, CNAC/MNAM/Dist. Réunion des Musées Nationaux/Art Resource, New York; p. 15
Hickey-Robertson, Houston; p. 6
Bill Jacobson; p. 14
Ellen Labenski; pp. 21–43
Kerry Ryan McFate; cover and p. 16
Ellen Page Wilson; p. 7, 12, 13 (fig. 7), 17

Design and Production:
PaceWildenstein

Color correction:
Motohiko Tokuta

Printing: Meridian Printing, East Greenwich, Rhode Island

ISBN: 978-1-930743-70-0